impspired@gmail.com

Cover illustration by Paul Holmes

ISBN: 978-1-915819-76-5

To my daughters Ailsa and Rosalind

OTHER TITLES BY IMPSPIRED

Maybury –
by Mary Farrell

Polygon -
by Domonique

Leviathan –
by Jae Jenkins Scott

Hyperbola -
by Shelly Norris

Spun Tales and Woven Words –
by North Coast Writers

The Mining Muse –
by Marc Darnell

Apartmentalized –
by Dan Flore III

FOREWORD

By James Simpson

An anthology to be explored, treasured and explored again. Robin's work embodies renaissance freshness and originality. His rural, south Down roots anchor him firmly to the natural world, while his soul soars on the wind, like the birds he loves. What a connection with the flora and fauna of Ireland, with the Mournes and the North Coast. With bluebells and primroses, sheep, cattle and faithful dogs. In this volume we walk below a wide sky. Joy and darkness, like the clouds, appear on a vast canvas.

Here we travel through buxom mountains, climb crags and peaks, stopping to marvel at their splendour, full of reflection. Human connection. Life, how it plays out, its transience, ecstasy, sadness. It's all there. Work, loss, time and tide.

This is a personal canon full of empathy and tenderness. *Knitting* is an intimate example. And all cast against the backdrop of art, music and literature from which so many allusions are easily drawn. His deft handling of Caravaggio, for example, and his own direct address to Christ, is almost shocking. Spirituality is everywhere. Acute observation is a given. Always there is compassion. He fails to condemn Judas outright, whose punishment was enough.

These poems should be read, time and again. They are moody but not bleak. Questioning but not despairing.

Delightful yet not naïve. Humorous but not cynical. There is harmony, cadence, honesty, and a resonating genuineness. What a gift.

A master of technique, Robin's metaphors flow. They are sustained and lingering. His imagery is adventurous and daring. He revels in rhyme and colour. Personifies love and wonder without recourse to sentimentality.

His facility for the right word in the right place is uncanny. Words come together, as though he were not the originator, but rather the conduit of some greater force. His deployment of alliteration verges on the spectacular. And all without ego.

Huge congratulations on a grounded, authentic, adventurous, compassionate, and highly relatable collection. A must read.

James Simpson was runner up in the Francis McManus Short Story Competition in 2013, and a finalist in the Irish Novel Fair of 2019. His anthology *Smokes and Birds* was published in 2021. He holds an MA in Creative Writing from Queen's University Belfast.

REVIEWS

Belying expectations generated by its title, The Shedding Gate is not limited in focus to rural and agricultural life. This potent collection deftly escorts the reader through a diverse range of topics, themes, styles and structures. These poems offer the reader a deeper understanding of the joys and wonders, losses and longings of being human.

Guided by Robin's sensitivity and skill we explore his thoughts on music, art, history, sport, bird watching, farm work and life experiences. This collection delivers nourishment for the soul throughout four thoughtfully curated themes.

Robin's poems weave together observations of nature and the farming world in a way that encourages consideration of their inherent beauty and wisdom. They reveal an instinctual connection to the landscape and anchor his worldview with a sense of place and belonging. A refined appreciation of art and music mirror the poet's love of language to leave a lingering sense of graceful reflection and a connection to something greater than ourselves.

This collection conjures memories of past times, a simpler world. Layers of delicate detail paint vivid events from a microsecond spent observing a bird in flight to a tracing of the passage of months and seasons to lifetime interests imbued with loving care.

Geraldine Fleming, Author of *Curiosity* and *Fractured Echoes* (2023). Both published by Impspired.

Robin's talent for planning and guiding walks through relatively unknown scenery and ancient monuments is greatly appreciated by those who have joined him. In this collection he takes us with him in words, sharing his appreciation with a lyricism that is truly gorgeous as his unfettered imagination brings humble hedgerow colours to life and celebrates the virtues of even the most common birds.

He has an extraordinary ability to move between the human and more-than-human worlds. A heroic father swoops like a falcon. March is personified as a ploughman struggling through uneven furrows while spring becomes a horse-whisperer. His primroses are introverted: he sees the wounds forming on the face of the bog as the turf is won – and lost.

And while there is no escape from the realities of mundane life, as he describes the passage of time Robin remembers to look for beauty in the most demanding of situations. Whether encountering the loss of memory, its unlooked-for resurgence, or even *the longships of dread,* there is delight to be had as we journey through the wilderness his poetry evokes.

Sue Steging, Winner of the Seamus Heaney Prize for New Writing, 2023

In this debut collection, Robin Holmes brings into sharp focus the landscapes and lifeways of rural Northern Ireland. Whether 'the Rawhide men' herding sheep from high pastures down to the accordion swing of the shedding gate, turfcutters with spade and grape poised to cut 'the black, carboniferous bog cake' or a host of primroses 'glittering/like Van Gogh's chandeliered stars', these are poems that evoke human endeavours and natural environments in vivid detail. Across sequences about wild birds, sports figures, musicians, and day-to-day objects (a banana, a bar of Pears soap), Holmes displays striking similes and metaphors that will leave readers seeing the world from inventive, invigorating angles. The collection features a selection of the poet's own black and white photographs, their rich tones and textures a visual complement to the poems' moods and preoccupations.

Kathleen McCracken, poet and former Lecturer in Creative Writing at Ulster University

In 'The shedding Gate' Robin Holmes has produced a gem of a book. The poems are precious and delicate, as fine, fresh and sparkling as a morning in spring. We are taken on a journey of exploration through worlds we thought we knew but which suddenly are seen from a new perspective. The familiar becomes wonderful. And we cannot rush through, we must stop, examine, consider and reconsider.

The poems have a deeply felt reverence for nature - smell it, taste it, touch it and suddenly be surprised by an unexpected metaphor that perfectly captures the essence of a tree, a flower, a bird in flight. There is an intimacy and delicacy to his observations that captures the underlying nature of his subject, all recorded in precise and meticulous detail. But there are warnings too, for this world is a fragile place and we must treat it with care.

These poems need to be read and re-read. Each reading will reveal new rewards and insight for the reader. And beneath is an underlying spirituality never overtly mentioned but hinted at in the petal of a flower, a leaf on a tree and the song of a bird.

Jimmy Milliken, Writer, Poet and author of Cracking The Air , Impspired Press, 2022.

When asked by Robin to pick just one poem of his to discuss, I at first considered the task impossible … until this one kept floating to the top. (AS IF page 35) In 2020, at the time when world movements were restricted, but Nature's generosity was not, from windows in our respective homes, one long glorious hedge of whin blossom filled our sight line. That hedge was the inspiration for this poem.

For me, this is Robin at his best, marrying artistic analogies and creative techniques with skillful mastery. His poetic eye sees and translates the world in such a distinctive way, it colours our own vision. His is a generous and perceptive view which fuses the essence of people, images, places and timelines with ease. In '*As If*', Irish hedgerows and ditches are unravelled and re-spun, handed over to the genius of Van Goth to embroider with an enchanted array of yellow hues. Once read, this original observation of Robins will always be the first thought of any reader on seeing a whin hedgerow.

Again and again throughout this Collection, we are gifted with his open heartedness in letting us share his insight. What a legacy these poems and photographs impart, what a truly adept visionary this man is. This is a Collection which bequeaths to us the unique world he sees for we readers to savour. For this, heartfelt thanks to you Robin.

Mary Farrell is a Creative Writing Facilitator in Northern Ireland, and the author of six books.

CONTENTS

EARTHSONG

PLAINSONG

BIRDSONG

EVENSONG

EARTHSONG

The Shedding Gate

1

All day a great gathering was taking place.
Sheep combed of Summer's sweet grass
from the high pastures of
The Pot of Kiviter, a dark glacial corrie,
Luke's Mountain, Clonachullion
down the valley of the Cascade River.
Sheep scattered everywhere,
like dandruff on a black gown.
The flock growing in size and shape,
as a rough snowball rolled on the ground.
Tom, James and myself, totally exhausted;
three teenagers, but worked as hard as the dogs,
clambering up and down slopes,
our lanky legs as good as stilts.

Sheep blaring, bleating,
ewes looking for lambs.
"Come Bye, Away in a hint, Lie Down"
the air thick with shouted commands.
Dogs racing, weaving, sitting.
their tongues wagging as extractor fans,
a great commotion of sight and sound,
as if Duffy's Circus had come to town.
And now the memory, still sharp, of
deep piles of purple heather, sunburn,
constant midge bites, flies, the smell of sheep dung.
Above us, and oblivious, the wingbeats of a skylark.

At Skillen's Cottage, the sheep
finally driven into an ancient bouldered pen.
unable to defy the flailing arms, the muttered curses of
Bill and Joe, well weathered mountain men.
My father presided over the shedding gate,
which swung to and fro in his hands,
like an accordion.
Deluded sheep rushed towards it, sensing freedom,
only to be betrayed into another pen.
Eventually all strays and stragglers removed,
only blue keeled sheep in our homogenous pen.
And then the long trek home.,
the procession slithered like a grass snake,
through forest tracks, country roads, traffic mayhem.
One landrover, two hundred sheep, three dogs,
and us, the Rawhide men.

2

I never saw Tom or James
on a Sunday.
On Monday mornings
pupils would emerge from
country lanes, small farms, prefab estates,
and coalesce, like sheep.
Half an hour together on the bus
our singular pen.
At Downpatrick we would diverge to
separate schools on separate hills,
the Red High and the Green.
Branded by our blazers,
we would pass through the shedding gate again.

THE BULL

Black, black bull
blackbird black,
pick the stars out of the night sky
with tweezers, that black.
Shaggy, rough haired mop top,
a Beatle bull.
a Galloway bull, gold ring in your nose.
You were born to breed, and breed
and spread your beef thickened brood.

Below the blue rippled curtain of the Mournes,
my father and I, foddering cattle
A khaki Land Rover wanders across fields
I am throwing out armfuls of hay.
Cows mob behind in a famished fury
their perspiration hanging,
A Will –o'-the-Wisp in the winter air.

Told to stay put, he departs
to look the bull, it seemed.
But minutes drag, boredom broadens
I shiver, and feel imprisoned, deserted.
I wander off to find him,
a fragile independence asserted.

Over barbed wire, into   a strange field,
did my red hair signify a matador
to this suddenly enraged, thunderous hulk?
His determination steaming, to remove me
out of his hallowed path.

From nowhere my falcon father swooped.,
clutching me in his arms, but taking
into his own torso
the gnarled globe of that
galloping Galloway's head.

THE BULL

2

After hospital, your long recovery.
your bedroom a curtained barracks.
a large sheet of hardboard arrived
to fit under your mattress.
You lay pinned on it, for weeks
a collector's butterfly,
deprived of the sun.

Most evenings you came downstairs, groaning.
On a wooden chair, in front of the fire,
a curious ritual emerged, my mother
unwrapped your mummified body.
Bandages eased off your chest.
then lapping around you again, she
created a clutching cloth corset, coercing
those ribs into position;
a Morris dance around
the May Pole of your mangled body.

You revived a little; some evenings,
from an opaque screen in the corner,
cowboys emerged; Rawhide, Wagon Train,
vast stampeding herds of cattle, on dusty plains.
Perhaps you imagined
you were Rowdy Yates again?

Once a fortnight your medication arrived
In a wooden crate, from Maginn's Bar.
Your doctor had ordered a bottle each day
"It's good for iron ", he would have said.
Some evenings though, when visitors arrived
there seemed enough medication for all.
You recited the parable of 'The Boy And The Bull',
as my mother cloaked her disdain.
It was not quite what she had wanted,
a stout- fuelled agrarian Sunday school.

I sneaked out to read the directions
on the brown bottles lining the table,
'Arthur Guinness and Sons
St James's Gate Dublin'.
It settled slowly into tall tumblers,
white headed when full,
but black, black, black.
black as a Galloway Bull.

MARCH

March, one foot in Winter, one in Spring,
a ploughman who walks unevenly.
He tramps in the furrow, shivering.
March, one foot in Winter, one in Spring
Primroses a dream, snowdrops withering,
your garden; a cold Gethsemane.
March; one foot in Winter, one in Spring,
a ploughman who walks unevenly.

March is war like; with mad hares sparring,
yet devoid of Aphrodite's charms.
The black furrow still needs harrowing
March is war like, with mad hares sparring,
still yearning for what the sun will bring.
Daffodils await, whilst the earth warms.
March is war like; with mad hares sparring,
yet devoid of Aphrodite 's charms.

The Slemish swineherd became a poet,
triolets extolled the Ttrinity
Using the March shamrock to show it,
the Slemish swineherd became a poet.
A new faith, he sought to bestow it,
mystery wrapped in simplicity.
The Slemish swineherd became a poet,
triolets extolled the Trinity.

BLUEBELLS

You will find them, deep in untrodden sunglades,
murmurings of bluebells, marvellous,
mesmerised in their own melancholy;
waving trumpet, trinket bell heads,
each a phial of lapus lazuli,
azure alchemy of blue blended
sea mist and sky scrapings.

Between tree trunks, they occupy with temerity
the rutted, corrugated earth,
glowing in glaucous gaze,
merging into becalmed lagoons.
Imbibe their scent, delicate, diaphanous
as a gauze of gossamer, reviving
the tiredest soul, the dankest lungs.

Charmed out of chilled soil by the leitmotif of
resurgent thrushes, ebullient blackbirds,
from dawn to dusk they surge
under a pebble-dashed wall of sound;
miniature mirrors,
capturing, reflecting
the blue vaulted sky.

Yet tread carefully, as if on holy ground,
soon this shall be the graveyard of beauty.
These glistening sapphires will lose their sheen,
shrivel and shrink into a bulbous underground,
a dessicated dreamland. The year marches on,
some gawdy impostor awaits in the wings,
ready to enthral the wayward traveller.

PRIMROSES

bypassed by the muses of Spring
they huddle in clusters
along hedgerows   river banks
untrodden places
for primroses are introvert
self-contained   they have no truck
with their gawdy cousins
they do not march as golden hosts
nor troop their own colour

they do not belong to architects
town planners   garden centres
pale and lemony   timorous
yet robust   they listen to Radio Three
and write poetry   scribbling lines
on their green striated leaves
soft as lamb's ears
if you care to linger
lower your head   their scent
more delicate and memorable
than the best Chanel

this time of year,
if you pass through
Glenballyemon Glendun
Cregagh Forest where
the woodpecker drills
they have peppered
for endless miles
the verges and hedgerows
their petaline beauty glittering
like Van Gogh's chandeliered stars

BALLERINA

Winter has passed for me, thankfully.
Months measured out with coal buckets,
weekend episodes of Nordic Noir,
an anaesthetised half-life of
thwarted ambition, frozen desire,
until spring's horse whisperer
spoke esoteric words to
winter's fractious winds and
Ferguson grey skies.
See what joy spring now brings;
a conjured ballerina,
waiting in the wings.

THE LAST OF THE TURF CUTTERS

I first met them in May,
as Spring came bursting in,
a dancer waiting in the wings.
The egg-yolk gorse sizzled
and lark song oscillated,
an overture for their arrival.
He arrived, a turf spade
sharpened, coated in linseed oil;
she with a long handled grape,
and their lunch, nestled
in a wicker basket.
His spade, really an earth chisel,
a scalpel to dissect
the black, carboniferous bog cake.
Her grape, a fork to convey
the slices to a heathered table.

They worked in unison,
his spade incising, horizontal thrusts,
the slurp, slap and squelch
of bog water, drooling
from the wounded face.
Left to right, lower and lower,
each piece removed with
nonchalance, whilst she
laid them out as soldiers

in regimental rows. Hours later,
as Wellington at Waterloo,
he surveyed the growing ranks,
proud of their industry, won
by their calloused guile.
Summer breezes, a glazing sun,
would perfect their molten treasure.

2

Came June and hope was not yet eroded,
each day was seized, a new symmetry
emerged, the turf castled as oblong stooks,
towers like Jenga, black fibrous sun catchers.
I met them again in July,
'It is not good ,' he sighed,
'not even two dry days in a row.'
The rain came, as a plague,
day after day, week after week,
their labours a diluvian debacle.
October, and the castles were
shrinking, sodden sponges,
a thousand passengers for whom
the train of summer never arrived.
Their Waterloo had become a Somme,
a sea of mud, a fetid harvest,

the turf spade resting on its rack,
the lean- to
    empty.

AS IF (A Reflection on Whin Blossom)

As if
an opportunist thief sneaked up
on the sleeping mid-day sun,
then stole his yellow cardigan,
snipped it with scissors,
unravelled all that golden wool,
before embroidering it into all
of the hedgerows and ditches
of Ireland.

As if
a deranged alchemist
devised a new recipe,
collected tons of daffodils,
primroses, buttercups,
dandelions and strained egg yolk,
pouring it into huge vats,
where it boiled and simmered
for days, before spraying it onto
all the hedgerows and ditches.
of Ireland

As if
I travelled back in time
to a street in Arles
a night café, a bad house
perhaps, and rescued Vincent
from a bottle of absinthe,

an argument with Gaugain
over a skinny woman.
'Come', I said, 'back to Ireland,
bring tubes of burnt umber,
cadmium yellow, come and paint
our hedgerows, our ditches
give them the immortality
you have bestowed on
sunflowers, wheatfields, gleaners.
There will be no crows,
no threatening skies.'
So he came and painted
all the hedgerows and ditches
of Ireland.

HEDGES

As coconut ropes, lying
across the decks of ancient ships,
or rigging, silhouetted against a sky
hedges unfurl across the land.
Walk closer, for they are
bloated green pythons
bulging and bursting,
havens for all life,
thickets of briar, bramble, blackthorn.
Fecund, fertile and furtive, they are
hangars for birds, nest boxes,
vast estates for insects,
bus stops for bees and butterflies.
Seasonally colourful, they enchant
with gorse perfumeries, delicate breezes of
honeysuckle and dog rose.
What are they, if not a Noah's Ark
for a flood which never came?

Once they provided a sanctuary
for the hunted fox, the hounded hare.
Shade too for the ploughman,
noonday rest for the weary reapers.
Within their sheltering branches
the Supertramp slept soundly,
beneath a duvet of goose feathered stars.

JOY

(After an invasion of migrating butterflies from Africa in 2019)

Painted Ladies,
parked, preening
worn out wings;
flimsy, yet fluttering
in diaphanous delight.
Saharan sojourners,
migrating marvels,
kaleidoscopic clansmen,
booked into
a wildflower meadow,
a butterfly's bothy.
Joy's indescribable sway
has landed today.
Tomorrow, as joys are wont,
they'll fly away.

SLIEVE DONARD AND THE CLOUDS

Each day Slieve Donard,
buxom of granite,
wearing her clouds; a model
on a bouldered catwalk.
From the Spring Collection,
Cumulus, puffed and floating
as tufts of bog cotton.
Summer, and Cirrus dangles,
a light, wispy neck scarf.
Autumnal days find her wearing
an inert greatcoat of mist.
Winter moon clouds
lie over her shoulders,
like a mink coat.

and always the light,
framed and fractured,
forceful and fragile,
fantailed sunlight
funnelling into vast
radiating spokes,
puncturing and prising.
Great searchlights
sweeping across
Zeppelin clouds,
raking the sky,
God's fingers,
Relativity speaking.

GREEN

Plastic

Tikka Masala
and a Diet Coke today,
tomorrow's choked whale.

Ice

Earth, our Titanic,
hitting the thawing icebergs
we have created.

Carbon

My Carbon Footprint,
complicit in fractious storms,
comes back to haunt me.

Windfarms

White fanged hillside mobs,
wind is their great dictator.
flailing endlessly.

ROASTED EARTH

Recipe of the Week

Before cooking, ensure your product is thoroughly defrosted.
Allow a decade for the glaciers at the Arctic and Antarctic regions to melt and flow freely.
Pierce the protective ozone layer with a sharp knife; greenhouse gases are equally effective.
Place the Earth in a carbon fuelled oven at 200 Degrees Centigrade.
(180 degrees Fan assisted) for thirty years.
Turn occasionally, once every 24 hours should be sufficient.
Baste with thunder storms, flash floods and localized torrents.
When fully cooked allow to stand for an hour.
Serve with intergalactic gravy, root planets and sautéd humans.

Remember to recycle any plastic containers.

PLAINSONG

Psithurism

For I have bathed in
the tides of forests,
as you may, each morning
in the chilled winter sea.
Not for me an electrocution
of the senses, a saline sledgehammer,
but a still undressing of the mind,
an exchange of clothes, a
putting on of the silken robes
of wildness, an imbibing
of the scent of pine, larch
and spruce, wild garlic;
the fermenting freshness
of all flora, each breath a
a purge into purity.

and whether with birdsong,
in spring's surging symphony,
or the strangulated lament of
a solitary winter straggler,
such accompaniment
delights always; audible
above the trampling underfoot
of twigs, squelch of leaf mould,
my steps in a bossa nova beat
with each breaking breath,
and always, always, the

regiments of upright trunks,
branches, leaves, swaying,
striving, straining towards
a celestial ceiling; recruiting
me to enlist with their
soft, seamless psithurism.

BEST

Twisting, writhing,

Goal,

until alcohol tackled,

the legend stumbled.

FRED DIBNAH

Bolton born and bred
reared in a foundry
inherited the spirit of
Stephenson and Brunel
steeplejack jack of all trades
boiler suited flat capped
Lennon spectacled
self taught but
oozed knowledge
charisma polished
with an oily rag
loved the pub
and a pint or two
travelled extensively
on his steam engine
Aveling and Porter, 1912
hands always black
with oil or coal
his world of grime
dovetailed onto television
crumpled political correctness
into his back pocket
unchanged by stardom
until cancer arrived
'Bloody hell '
blew a rivet in his boiler
thought nowt of it at first
but were only thing
he could not fix or understand

A SHORT POEM ABOUT USSAIN…

laconic, languorous, wind jockey
human spring, compressed so tightly
mimicking Mohammed Ali
rewriting Relativity
vanishing into the vortex
of his own velocity

…BOLT

ROONEY

Nani sends in a high cross from the right,
Rooney is hovering, like a kestrel,
surveying the ball's elliptical flight,
but then he's a bloodhound, hot on the smell.
Spinning on his axis, a scissors kick,
spectacular, exquisite in it's bliss;
arrogant in ambition, brazen, slick.
His legs thrust like pistons, crying 'Watch this '.
The ball flies on its curved trajectory,
past Hart's fingertips, into the net,
a stunning, swirling path of ecstacy.
Eruptions of elation; and regret.
Rooney is a King Kong, punching his chest.
A gladiator who knows he is the best.

THE BROAD STONE

Broad Stone, on the Long Mountain,
You are a Court Cairn, resembling a Portal Dolmen.
Before the Pyramids you were, and
after the Moon Landings you remain.
Your capstone is a timeless table, a
stone diaphragm, receiving sunlight and moonlight.
Galaxies and nebulae talk to you, comets sing,
you wear rainbows as a necklace.

The attrition of wind and rain
fails to erode your silent majesty.
Archaeologists and anthropologists
conjecture on your meaning,
but to me it is enhanced
by subjectivity; my finitude
besides your longevity,
a sense of numinous awe,
the dwindling to a pinprick
of my own significance.

My visits to you therefore
stand as pilgrimages, whether
through cloisters of clouds,
vast halls of mist. Cloaked in
remoteness, you play hide and seek
with the contours, the swivelling light.
I like it best in May, when you dwell

within the blandishments of Spring.
Resting against your orthostat,
a diva skylark sings for me,
Whitethorn burns its incense and
from somewhere in the dark forest,
that African visitor casts
his two note spell over
your nonchalant, granite grin.

A BANANA POEM

half past five
on the deadline night,
I've nothing specular
or spectacular to write.
but here's something
of which I am capable,
a banana poem,
to bring to the table.
two minutes of
intense nutrition,
filled with similes
and alliteration.
a banana poem,
neither banal
or anal,
a little slice
from the
Tower of Babel.
something modest
to revel in,
and when you're finished,
throw away the skin.
my banana poem?
it's biodegradable.

SO WE MEET AGAIN MY HEARTACHE

after Melody Gardot

so we meet again my heartache,
at this table set for two.
The à La Carte, for broken hearts,
the Specials, all prepared by you.

so we meet again my heartache,
each restless night I toss and turn.
No blissful sleep, no kisses deep,
how you prolong my dark sojourn.

so we meet again my heartache,
with memories which sear me through.
The dagger glides, with words inscribed
'I once loved you.'

so we meet again my heartache,
is there no place I can go?
My grief is stretched, in black fishnets,
one mawkish last tango.

and so we meet again my heartache,
like some black raven from above.
Here to haunt me, still you taunt me.
then dance me to the end of love.

OTTILIE

Ottilie, Ottilie,
singing the Blues for me
Ottilie, Ottilie,
singing the Blues for me.
From the green hills of Comber
to the dark Mississippi.

Ottilie, Ottilie,
Blues running through your veins
Ottilie, Ottilie,
Blues running through your veins.
From the bright lights of Soho
to the soft Chicago rain.

Well your full moon eyes
and that pile driving voice.
Yes those full moon eyes
and that pile driving voice.
When you sang the blues,
you made us all rejoice.

Ottilie, Ottilie,
some said you got it wrong.
Ottilie, Ottilie.
some said you got it wrong.
A white woman singing,
singing the black man's song.

Some said you had troubles,
this mean world treated you unkind.
Yes you had those troubles,
this world can be so unkind.
Troubles in your body,
and troubles in your mind.

Ottilie, Ottilie,
they snuffed your candle out.
Ottilie, Ottilie,
they snuffed your candle out,
and no, nobody loves you
when you're down and out.

Ottilie, Ottilie,
you still lived out your dream.
Ottilie, Ottilie,
the best I've ever seen.
With Lady Day and Amy,
to the streets of New Orleans.

OTTILIE PATTERSON (1932 to 2011) One of Northern Irelands greatest Jazz and Blues Singers. Sang with the Chris Barber Band in the 1950' and 60's.

PEARS

You fit into my hand
like a skimming stone,
my forefinger curled,
ready to hurl you
into water, where you belong.
Yet I cherish your transparency,
your tactile beauty;
a burnished chestnut,
gracing the basin,
stranded as a glacial erratic.
Kneading you between my palms,
you give generously,
a soft, saturated Cuckoo- Spit.

On overtime in the bath,
you glide over the continent
that is my body, exploring
inlets, climbing ridges.
going to the places
only lovers know.
Suddenly you escape my clutch,
becoming a slithering eel,
skating invisibly on
the delph sea floor.

Weeks pass and you diminish
into a shrivelled tongue,
a spawned salmon,
dying on the gravel bed.
Your pristine replacement
awaits in its box.
Skin and water have written
the libretto of your life,
the original
Soap Opera

STOWAWAY

You arrive in a soft, wafting breeze,
an interruption of the assumed stillness,
but then, in an eerie whisper,
you announce your intentions,
a wolf howling into an echo-less night.
A full moon, hanging like a glitter ball,
is suspended between the clouds,
waiting for the earth to dance.
Soon the un -tethered world
will begin to slip and scud.
I try to lock the door, but you
grab it, playing it as an accordion.
Your banshee wail is merely a prelude,
within an hour you have chosen Gale Force.
A mad conductor, your baton directs
the waving boughs of leafless trees,
now violins in your unfinished symphony…
'Alllegro, Allegro' you shout, as you outspeed
them, snapping their brittle bows.
Upstairs, I open opposing windows
to let you in, briefly. You fill
the billowing curtains as a mainsail.
Against my skin you press a chilled kiss.
Cosseted within cotton sheets, I listen

to your plaintive lullabies.
I am hiding deep within the hull,
a stowaway in the storm's crescendo.
In the morning, the world is flat, punctured,
placid. In furrowed fields a gnarled tree
lies horizontal, an upturned centipede,
its branches spiked and speared into earth…
Your scrawling, backhand signature
is everywhere, the gale's graffiti.
I miss you, my tall ship
now lying in the doldrums...

TREBLE CLEF

Beethoven

Your Third, Fifth and Ninth,

tortured symphonic genius,

deafness hearing joy.

Chopin

Consumed consumptive,

heart bleeding into nocturnes,

keys played by snowflakes.

Debussy

Listened to moonlight,

shimmering arpeggios,

unrequited love.

BIRDSONG

ROBIN

''Look at me, look at me,' you say,
as you come hopping around
with your James Cagney swagger
and oozing impudence.
Your paper clip legs are merely stems
to your bright flower, for you are
a follower of Prometheus,
carrying a hot coal on your breast,
a glowing charcoal ember,
fanned brighter by Winter's ancient bellows.
In your tabloid, tinsel world,
you are a born poser, perching on
post boxes, garden spades, door handles.
Snow scenes are your favourite,
you shift cards and calendars by the truckload.
Together with swans and donkeys,
you have made being twee respectable.

Yet I like you best
when I do not see you;
as on a frost clamped day,
from a ghost of a tree,
your song bursts forth,
bayonetting the death camp gloom.
Momentary, mellifluous, melodic,
like an Arabian flute, precise as a piccolo.
On such occasions you are a joy bringer,
a hot Port to all the senses.

I imagine it was for more prosaic reasons,
my mother named me after you.

DOVES

doves

from above

doves elemental

doves gentle

doves wooing

doves cooing

doves resting

doves nesting

doves breeding

doves feeding

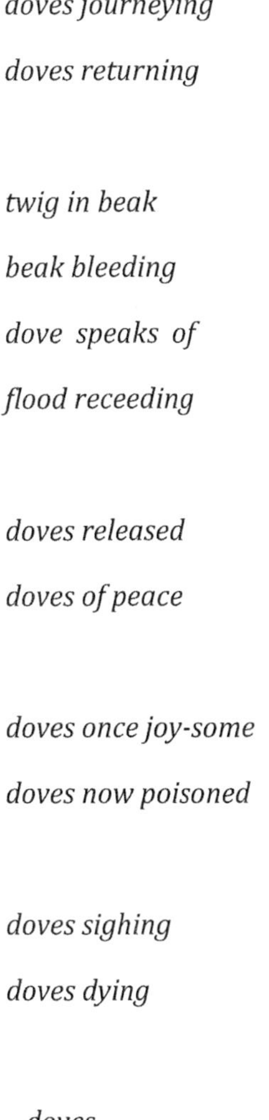

doves journeying

doves returning

twig in beak

beak bleeding

dove speaks of

flood receeding

doves released

doves of peace

doves once joy-some

doves now poisoned

doves sighing

doves dying

doves

House Sparrow

Tincture of twig and tree bark,

smudged with charcoal,

you flutter in, chirping

three cheeps and the truth.

Impudent, quarrelsome, you

once shared the eaves

of our houses, until

our need for insulation,

perfection, ousted you

to hedgerows, dilapidation.

Your numbers rapidly dwindling,

charitable donations assuage

our occasional guilt.

Relatively un-blessed, neither

the fighter pilot glamour

of soaring, striking raptors.

nor the elegaic eloquence

of sumptuous songbirds,

neither Fabritius's palatte

of prized, caged finches,

nor, for you, the odes

of Keats and Shelley;

just one of the proletariat,

a plain Jane, expendable,

except, two to the penny,

you are

a patent of Providence,

each fall recorded

in the annals of God.

Magpies

Not everything is black and white,
but you are.
The frenetic flurry
of your short haul flights,
carrying your tail like a ladder.

Your penchant for playing
Russian roulette with road kill,
then, engorged with one last peck,
you rocket off in front of cars,
intoxicated with the thrill.

A name synonymous for being
a collector and a hoarder.
Your nest lined with trinkets, silver and gold,
perhaps you have
an Obsessive Compulsive Disorder.

You arrive bringing portents of doom
and percolating superstition.
Medieval artists located you
at the Crucifixion,
but not the Resurrection.

Subject of myriad nursery rhymes
which children recite, without fuss.
'Maggoty pie
Maggoty pie,'
you are a feathered abacus.

Starring roles in Rossini's Overture
and Monet's Winter Landscape
have made you a cultural icon.
A black robed cleric of the ominous,
but no Medieval bygone.

Not everything is black and white,
nor precisely as it appears.
You are a darkroom print,
an enlargement of our
deepest, unsettled fears.

A Buzzard Rising

'Keer kee-eera'
as always I hear you first,
you announce your presence discretely,
as I search for your silhouette.
Who crucified you onto the sky,
blue as an Aegean sea?.
Four feathers, on each wing tip,
clasp the heavens,
yet you circle perfectly,
as if pinned to the invisible sails
of a Dutch windmill.
Or do you tread air,
harnessed to a walk mill in the clouds?
Your mime mesmerises me,
masking the motionless minutes,
until a change of plan.
Several wing beats prove you are still alive,
as you move, with nonchalance,
onto another thermal.

So what shall I call you?
No venereal noun for you,
no exaltation of larks, no parliament of owls
no murmuration.
You despise the collective.
Your heart is a lonely hunter.
You are a Lindberg, an Amelia Earheart
crossing continents, desolate oceans.
You hunt for your prey
like Von Richthofen,
your victories etched
on the fuselage of your solitude.

A Buzzard Fallen

There you were,
grounded, hogging a Slieve Croob road;
statuesque, like a turkey,
immobile and stunned.
My car could have killed you,
road kill for a murder of crows.

Walking towards you,
I was mesmerised by your camouflage.
Your beak, as curved as a sickle,
your talons, a pair of grapple hooks, your eyes
as brown and polished as saddle leather.
You were a hunting machine,
a mottled Messerschmitt,
now downed and doomed.

My benevolent intentions were anathema to you.
I, too, had become a predator.
You stuttered, fluttered and flapped;
making it to a gate top.
No veterinary practice could save you;
not for you the cushioned domesticity of cats and dogs.

And then, one final flight.
You crash landed into the dark hedge,
a thicket of thorns would become your tomb.
In the distance the granite tors of
Binian, Bearnagh, Ben Crom
glinted in the fading sun.
I hoped you would die, dreaming
of the thermals you once had graced.

Gothic Stuff

With your frying pan face,
amidst an Elizabethan ruff,
those teddy bear eyes
and all that Gothic stuff;
ghostly moon flights,
night vision and radar,
stealthily stalking mice,
a white Darth Vader.
Return wise owl,
with your fabled charms;
replenish our lives,
replenish
our
barns.

TWO LAPWINGS

Seeking a corner   of real estate
    to build an   alluvial apartment,
        a brittle bothy   to   brood and breed
            Their sartorial crests   are ancient antennae,
                attuned to another   world   the ebb and flow
                                of moon and tide
.   of moon and
                                        tide

Intoxicated by   Spring's seismic surge
    they launch into   air sky- skipping
        a delirious display   of aerial abandonment
                barnstorming bravado   claws latching in mid-air
                            a flamboyant flamenco
                                    of flight.

finally the sky
drilled and gouged by
the curvature of their wings
collapses in on itself
in smithereens
of awe

SENTINEL

Grey Heron

Silent sentinel of the sedges,
wading, watching, waiting
for what might appear.
Your beak, your neck,
blend imperceptibly
into a two eyed spear.
But yet, when startled,
you can hardly fly at all,
your wings a torn out
    letter M
you rise   you fall.

        You are
a Buddha amongst birds,
the antithesis of commotion,
        living a life,
        as you do,
      in slow motion.

Starlings

Strutting storm troopers speckled Spartans
opportunist criminals of the avian underworld
stupendous flock flying in unison
such murmurations help me forgive
your blitzkrieg on the breadcrumbs

Whooper Swans

Airborne trumpeters
white arrowhead sky–splitting
wings gulping chilled air

Recital

buoyant Mistle Thrush
sensing warmer days
recites his back catalogue

Swallows, an addendum.

I told you before about the swallows,
the frenetic, frenzied zig-zag of their flight,
the Heathrow they maintained
in the old byre, their pimpled nests
adhering to the rafters like clams.
But this is September and they have sensed
an equinox approaching, an equatorial pull,
so now they are gone. If they arrived
as the gift wrapping of spring,
they are gone in the mournful wake
for summer, leaving a tangible silence;
the buildings they once invigorated,
deserted as a famine village.

Yet there must be a somewhere
their flight still delights.
As the muezzin drifts from tall minarets,
they weave across elephant grass,
Saharan dust still in their wings.

EVENSONG

Knitting

In your cupboard, amidst
the acquired detritus of ninety years,
a ball of wool, navy blue and
starling speckled.
A Valentine's heart
pierced by two needles.
Each evening,
after a frugal tea,
you sat, with a widow's silence
knitting stitches   casting on,
knitting stitches   casting on,
knitting stitches   casting on;
the snick of needles,
regular as a loom.
Your hands then,
arthritic, hacked and calloused,
yet each pendulum evening
was measured out by inches,
until a lengthening
snake of a scarf touched the floor.
You produced scarves
for those you loved;
distributing them, as if
the Queen, on a Maundy Thursday,
until one evening
you put the wool down, forever.
When was that?

Your mind seemed to enter a tunnel,
dense with mist, with fog.
Your life got stuck
in reverse gear.
We heard the rasping of clutch plates
and feared, as your coordination collapsed;
the slow disintegration of
an ordered world.
And so you spent
the next decade
knitting memories,
giving us sepia toned scarf stories
to keep the cold away.

Calendars

Juvenile in January,
dangling on walls
as fresh washing on a line,
a twelve eyed ambassador of the year,
flaunting bright, bespoke images
of art, landscape, chosen heroes.
Each month a white chessboard
of pristine days, soon to be chosen,
ticked, usurped by appointments;
a lithograph of the predictable,
'God willing, if I'm able, touch-wood',
No room for the unforeseen, immunised
against the broken world, each page
excited with the prospect of its
own brief fondle with time.

Yet they are the poor relations to
diaries, monuments, headstones;
a gaudy paper flower, bleached
with the seasons passing, into irrelevance.
December, and the dandelion calendar
has shed most of its scribbled days.
Some exit into treasure drawers,
others into the Hades of blue bins.
The mind does its own recycling,
waiting for the
ragged
revenant
of
memory.

About Time

On my wrist always,
a metallic time machine,
its seconds hand goose steps
around the silver perimeter,
a beast of burden, trapped
in an endless walkmill.
The minutes hand moves slower
but not imperceptibly,
it is sometimes seen to jump
as a trout might, catching flies.
The hour hand governs life,
regulates necessities; we watch it
as a beautiful stranger in a crowd.
Time never falters, never chokes,
running its own marathon.
Unable to outpace it, we drop
on the roadside, needing pit stops,
before curling into the unconsciousness
of sleep, declaring a curfew for dreams.
Time's alarm reawakens, hurling us
into the clasp of another day.

Lifetime

As trapped sand trickles
through the aperture
of the hourglass,
governed by gravity,
our days drip,
intravenously, into
weeks, months and years;
the seasons merely
colouring the clock face.
Some days, marinaded in joy,
seared with sorrow,
carve themselves on
the Ogham Stone of memory.
Time mauls its own metaphors,
a time to scatter stones
and a time to gather them.
We are timekeepers,
running on timetables.
Having the time of our lives,
our time is soon spent,
Times Winged Chariot
flying through the dust
of
a

lifetime.

DEATHS AND MARRIAGES
For The District Of
REGISTRAR
DEPUTY REGISTRAR
Days And Hours of
Every TUESDAY And FRIDAY

A VIGIL

Upstairs, in your nursing home,
the hours are laden with a saturated stillness.
My hand reaches through the steel cot sides
to hold yours, an umbilical cord of love.
Our roles reversed, the hands that once
nursed, rocked and fed me.
You are walking through the valley,
the valley of long shadows.
The warmth of your hand oscillates,
a tentative tachograph of life.
When you squeeze my hand
it is a Morse Code, saying
"I am still here".

Outside, at dusk each evening, the rooks
migrating home, travelling
as if on long, pencilled, parallel lines.
Some in flocks, others are lonesome stragglers,
stricken bombers limping home;
their black wings rise and fall like oars,
gulping the air of the gloaming.
In the distance a rookery,
where leafless branches strangle the setting sun.
A vast, raucous, cawing cacophony
evanesces into an eternal evensong.

One evening you too became restless,
battling for air, morphine swirling through;
until your breathing dropped to a whisper,
and then you flew away.

Girona

On that night, the creaking, cracking and crumpling
of timbers: hull, bow and stern.
Masts scythed by the wind, falling as trees,
your sinking as assured as gravity.
Sailors diving into their salted graves,
dug by a calamitous sea.
Lying for generations in the ocean's tomb,
your timbers rotted, pulped and marinaded
in the bitter brine: the elements pestle and mortar
grinding away your destiny.

Until the Belgians came in 1968: a flotilla,
not an armada, armed with wet suits,
flippers, aqualungs, searchlights and cameras.
Fingers filtering through the slime, into
seaweed purses, gravel pouches, rocky chasms.
The ocean yielded up her secret hoard of
necklaces, brooches, amulets, torques,
salamanders of gold and
an engagement ring, enigmatic, engraved,
which, when cleaned and polished, began to sing
a song unheard for centuries,
' I have nothing more to give Thee'.
A melody composed, notated and scored
by the black, mournful, basalt sea.

FEBRUARY

In Memory of Eveline McCullough 1954-2016

February, the snowdrops shivering,
white hooded nuns, Winter's contemplatives;
their devotions still the earth's quivering.
February, the snowdrops shivering,
as welded snowflakes; the frost delivering,
just when the earth had nothing to give.
February, the snowdrops shivering,
white hooded nuns, Winter's contemplatives.

For a hallowed hour, in which you were here,
your camera clicked relentlessly.
To you, Spring would never reappear.
For a hallowed hour, in which you were here,
you seized the day, dispelling fear
and danced joyously with the snowdrop's glee.
For a hallowed hour, in which you were here,
your camera clicked relentlessly.

The snowdrop avenues, where once you walked,
retrieve their glory annually.
Hope has triumphed, though despair has stalked
the snowdrop avenues, where once you walked.
Unafraid of your future, you never baulked,
ending your days courageously.
The snowdrop avenues, where once you walked,
retrieve their glory annually.

Pages of the Sea, Murlough

I watched you die a second time,
as the impatient tide lapped
over your boots, your breeches,
your tunic, each successive wave
going over the top, as you had often done
into the fury of No Man's Land.
Today you died in the tide's soft caress,
your khaki, sand silhouette sifted
and smoothed into oblivion.
Your first death, who knows how?
a lone sniper? or did your body become
mincemeat, shredded by machine gun fire,
artillery shells, your lungs gasping for air
through clouds of cordite and chlorine?
Passchendaele, what a misnomer for
the airless abbatoir where your body
was flushed into the mud, grave- less.
No Thankful Village for your return, but
today a gratitude of sorts. Our raked silhouettes
rinsed away, but your memory outlives
the tide's fickle surge. If only I could tell you,
even the Mournes stood to attention.

A BETRAYAL

after *The Taking Of Christ* by Caravaggio, 1602.

This is the moment of betrayal, frightened faces floodlit with
moonlight and lanterns, flushed from a burrow of darkness,
brows engraved with the agony which first festered in Gethsemane.
Christ, your eyes are closed, you dare not look at your betrayer,
the smack of his lips, wet as a slug, poisoned with hypocrisy.
Your hands are clasped, as if still in prayer, your fingers
dovetailed, passive as a lamb, ready to be roped.
Judas, your forehead striated, years of living in the desert sun,
the stress of managing the communal purse, you gaze
away from your adversary, imagining now a silvered future.
Three soldiers, manacled in their own armour,
black iron growling, moulded helmets and visors,
grasping for their helpless prey.
There is no miracle to overcome such malevolence.

Michelangelo Meresi da Caravaggio,
lantern holding in your own picture,
you eschewed bucolic idylls, cherubic babes,
the tinselled iconography of haloed madonnas.
You arranged tableaus of common people
with dirt and grit realism, eye catching
as a grocer's window, visceral and violent.
Painting chiaroscuro, you perfected two extra brushes,
dipped in light and darkness, whittled to perfection
in the grim, turbulent cellar of your own life.
Yet in the silver streaks of light gleaming
on polished armour, you created subtle mirrors,
hoping we might catch glimpses of ourselves,
our own
unlit
betrayals.

HEARTFELT

Embedded below my rib cage,
a thumping, throbbing underground station,
where blood is squeezed and squashed
into arterial carriages, stops at all vital organs,
lungs, kidneys, liver, brain, St Pancreas.
Red line, *Central,* travelling from brain to toe,
Blue line, returning veins, *District or Circle,*
services almost every second, with
ventricles, valves, chambers, aorta,
all pumping and purring, as smoothly
as a Rolls Royce Silver Cloud.

and though held in marvel and awe,
hearts decay and age. Substances and stress
erode efficiency, lines become blocked
with the leaves of cholesterol,
boulder clots derail, sometimes fatally.
The heart's pendulum loses precision,
arrhythmias arrive, the heart stutters.
Surgeons, like plumbers, hover
with a bulging tool box;
pacemakers, valves, stents,
ingenious space age technologies,
the heart being more mapped than the moon.

Yet the heart exists, as poets know it,
and often show it, within a mysterious ether;
call it persona, psyche, soul or spirit.
Hearts can be broken,
and sometimes mend.
The heart is a lonely hunter,
everybody has a hungry heart.
Wordsworth's heart leapt at the sight of a rainbow,
Dylan, deserted, felt a cork screwed on his heart.
Grief and sorrow pierce the heart like briars,
separation and divorce wrap the heart in barbed wire.

All euphemisms belie, that
the heart of the matter is,
the heart is more, so much more
than matter.

DOGGED

Survival and two decades have chewed away
the bone of his life
his once clear Perspex eyes
are now frosted marbles
once the whole olfactory world
was on heat to his nose led explorations
now he is congested with the slurry
of his own pee and saliva
his teeth are more Polyfilla than pearl
as he gently chews his milk-soaked meal
he slopes and slides around the garden
before sitting like a Sphinx
becoming a statue of himself
as an adolescent he was happy on a straw bed
sharing the old byre with the swallows
now he has become a house pet
splayed on a fireside cushion
he twitches and snores
perhaps he is dreaming of the days when
he could stare out a herd of bullocks
nose to nose through a fence   or
outflank a shapeless cloud of ewes

I think often of the day we met
him abandoned, dumped and mangey
following me tentatively his origins
as shrouded as the Mourne mist
from which he emerged
did I rescue him
or did he rescue me?
now it seems
we both grow old together
a dogged double- act
without a lead or license

SOMETHING ABOUT SEPTEMBER

Today the air is soft, serene,
with a languorous lilt,
a sense of ending
which could be sliced.
Maudlin clouds drift,
huddled across the sky.
The air smells of burning leaves,
yet there is no fire.
The earth, cooling,
moves in whispered tones,
no longer bulbous,
no longer raucous.
In stubbled fields
round bales rest like spools,
a hydraulic harvest
has happened overnight,
The ancient symmetry has died,
hands no longer sting, or bleed
making stooks, thatching ricks,
feeding the endless hunger
of threshing machines.
Harvest bows are pinned
to the walls of museums,
churches are undecorated.
The seasons, diluted,
blend as imperceptible
as the salmon,
no longer spawning
in the stained rivers.

Autumn Manna

October, limping towards the year's demise
yet resplendent in russet robes;
you are wedded to the wild, west wind
spreading your bronzed, scorched leaf confetti.
You have enticed my daughters and me
to stray into these ancient woods, and
in trespassing, inherit what is ours.
Our hands delve into the dank mulch
of leaves, to find our treasure;
a storm fall of chestnuts, Autumn Manna.
Some still in the foetal warmth
of spiked kernels, others lying alone,
glistening, staring through buff, bloated eyes.
Obsessively we sift,
with a Klondike zeal,
for their luscious sheen.

Horse chestnuts, like chestnut mares,
rich and redolent;
burnt, burnished, shining
as a dance floor.
Rolling in our palms, as
deep nuggets of Pears Soap;
your browns, your reds,
your polished globes
become our ware.
Our pockets bulge
with your pebbled hulk,
a cunning theft as
we homewards skulk.

NENDRUM IN NOVEMBER

for Kim Rhiannah.

A thousand years of wind and rain
have not effected it's dissolution.
Gable ends, the stump of a round tower,
enclosing walls, suggest a former glory.
A sundial no longer governs monastic life
but chides today's pensive pilgrim.
Wire brush winter trees roughen the horizon,
as the clotted cream orb of the Super Moon
rises slowly, as if being inflated, yet
invisibly tethered to the earth.
Looking south, the tin foil silver of the lough
shivers and shimmers in the twilight.
The reflected light of lonely farmsteads,
moored yachts and a lightship is
a tachograph, oscillating across the water.

All is glistening in this gloaming.
On a summit I stand behind you,
encircling you in my arms.
The Vikings have come and gone,
and our Vikings too,
rogue cells, burst arteries,
the longships of dread sailing
into our lough- side contentment.
Yet, like this monastery, we have survived
and tonight exult in the lough's evensong;
the soft, caressing whispers of the tide
against a shingled shore,
the distant cack and caw
of roosting rooks,
diving into their own delirium.

Amongst the Ancients

after Cornfield by Moonlight, with the Evening Star, c1830
by Samuel Palmer

Enthroned within a black leather sky,
a crescent moon, resting as a sliver
of lemon, beckoning to the Evening Star;
a suspended sisterhood of radiance.
Light trails from the moon, as wisps of straw,
falling from an overloaded wagon.
An archaic shepherd, bent in reverence
with crook and dog, follows an illuminated path,
through, in my surmise, the field of his labour.
Earlier, his body swaying with the
slash of sickle, the swish of scythe, whilst
others laid out straw bands, before
their encircling arms formed and
bound the fecund, bulging sheaves.
Now that which was reaped under a gaudy,
scorching sun, is caressed and moonstruck.
Beyond, in the dense forested slopes, trees bask
in the ethereal glow as burnished florets of light.
Through the woods, secret paths to Shoreham
where The Ancients imbibe Virgil and Blake.
In a landscape beguiled with a soft phosphorescence,
all aisles converge in this moon-gold field,

a pilgrim's way into the transcendent,
a nocturne yearning for the numinous.
With Yellow Ochre, Cadmium,
Raw Umber, the distillation of moonlight
is as complete as the stooked harvest.
The artist's vision is serenely displayed,
'dream of a dream, and shadow of a shade.'

December Diary

in a time of Covid

dusk approaching
deep blue sky
dimmed to indigo
faint stars venture
out of
dressing rooms
new crescent moon
curved
as a curlew's bill
banana bright
looking down
on a
coughing   choking
Earth
billions masked
billions in burrows
fleeing mutations
as if
Herod has reordered
the Slaughter of
the Innocents

moon brightening
sliver of
shivering light
moon reposing
against the
dark throw
of night
shedding a tear
for sister Earth
such beauty
framed by sorrow
Clair de lune
drowned
in a
requiem

The Road to Nowhere

It seemed like the road to nowhere,
the road I would always choose;
tired of the streets of somewhere,
tired of yesterday's news.
Time for the depths of the forest,
time for the desert's harsh sands,
a breeze on my face, grit on my toes,
the soul's relentless own plans.
With no compass or map to guide me,
only the impromptu desires of the heart;
sometimes the road to nowhere,
is the very best place to start.

It seemed like the road to nowhere,
choking with nettles and thorns;
through perilous snares, immeasurable snares,
exacting but forlorn.
Though often the road to nowhere
may seem like the back of beyond,
such unknown paths may lead you
to the peace of Walden's still pond.
When you reach the desired destination,
through days of hardship and distress,
your delight was really the journey,
your tonic, the great wilderness

ACKNOWLEDGEMENTS

As with Newton's well used analogy, I feel I have only arrived here by standing on the shoulders of giants. Indeed, there are many worthy of mention.

Firstly, I would like to thank Paul Holmes for providing the specially commissioned cover illustration and all of the pencil drawings inside. The watercolour of the Mournes vividly sets the atmosphere for many of the poems and the bird drawings are stunning.

A huge debt of gratitude is due to Steve Cawte, editor of Impspired, without whom this book would not have existed. His editorial skills have been tested to the limit by my wish to include a series of Black and White film photographs with some of the poems. As always, he has come up trumps!

I would also like to thank my fellow North Coast Writers facilitator Mary Farrell. Since we started the group in 2017, she has been a constant source of inspiration and guidance. With this publication she greatly assisted me in learning new computer skills and her practical help in completing the Masterfile has been invaluable.

In 2016 I joined a Creative Writing Class at Flowerfield Arts Centre, led by Bernie Mc Gill. The inspiration and nurturing provided by her set me off on this writing journey; at one point when I felt like giving up, a crucial email from her put me back on course. Thank you so much, Bernie.

From that time a number of Writing friends have walked alongside me and their support, enthusiasm and encouragement has been very precious. I mention here Jim Simpson, Jimmy Milliken, Brendan Magee, Geraldine Fleming, Sue Steging and Tom Adair.

I would like to thank the Community Arts Partnership for the many courses and workshops they have offered, especially those taken by the following poets: Stephen Sexton, Moyra Donaldson, Stephanie Conn and Emma Must. A special word of thanks to Dr Kathleen Mc Cracken, whose encouragement and guidance has been immensely helpful. I must mention too, Paul and Amy from The Bangor Literary Journal. You provided an exciting window of opportunity for new writing and your competitions and special readings were always so enticing.

Two friends in particular have helped me with practical issues concerning the photography and also providing digital scans of the cover illustration and the bird drawings. To Kenneth Wood and Derek Simpson, a heartfelt thank you.

There are probably many others I have failed to mention but I cannot close without mentioning two teachers of English Literature long ago in my High School days. They instilled within me a great love and appreciation of poetry and writing. Thank you, Mervyn Smith and Betty Lascelles; the seed you planted has come to fruition in this book.

ACKNOWLEDGEMENT OF FIRST PUBLICATION

As if *(A reflection on Whin Blossom)* Shortlisted for the Eighth Annual Bangor Poetry Competition, and published in the *Bangor literary Journal* December 2020.

Bluebells Published in the CAP Poetry in Motion Anthology *Heartland*, 2021.

Primroses Published in the CAP Poetry in Motion Anthology *Compass*, 2023.

Slieve Donard and the Clouds Published in the Anthology *Irish Hares and Sea Horses,* Impspired 2022.

Psithurism Published in *The Bangor Literary Journal,* Issue 14, Spring 2021

So We Meet Again, My Heartache Published in the anthology *Spun Yarns and Woven Words,* Impspired 2023

Treble Clef Published in the anthology *Irish Hares and*

Sea Horses, Impspired 2022.

Stowaway Shortlisted for the Seventh Annual *Bangor Poetry Competition* and published in *The Bangor Literary Journal,* 2019

Two Lapwings Published in the CAP Poetry in Motion Anthology *Vision,* 2020.

A Recital Shortlisted for *The Bangor Literary Journal's annual Forty Words Competition* and published in 2022.

Swallows, an addendum Published in the CAP poetry in Motion Anthology *Threshold,* 2022

Knitting Commended in *The Bangor Literary Journal's Sixth Annual Poetry Competition* and published in 2018.

A Vigil Published in the anthology *Irish Hares and Sea Horses,* 2022, published by *Impspired Press.*

Girona Published in the CAP Poetry in Motion Anthology *Resonance,* 2018.

Murlough, Pages of the Sea Published in the CAP Poetry in Motion Anthology *Find,* 2019.

A Betrayal Published in the CAP Poetry in Motion anthology *Heartland,* 2021

Heartfelt Published in *Love, Loss and Cardiac Issues, 2022, Impspired Press.*

Nendrum in November Published in *The Memory of Snow,* a selection by Gaynor Kane for *The Bangor Literary Journal,* December 2019

Amongst the Ancients Published in the CAP Poetry in Motion Anthology *Vision,*2020.

ABOUT THE ARTIST

Award winning artist Paul Holmes A.S.U U.W.S, born on the Antrim Coast, takes inspiration for his paintings from the beautiful landscapes of Ireland, both north and south. His work is now collected internationally and can be seen in galleries throughout the island of Ireland.

Paul has held the offices of President of the Arts Society of Ulster and Vice president of the Ulster Watercolour Society.

NOTES ON THE PHOTOGRAPHY

I have included a selection of my own photographs to both supplement and complement a number of the poems. At first, I felt rather tentative and ambivalent about this project, but seeing the two come together in print has greatly encouraged me. Like poetry itself, black and white photography can show but not tell, and it can suggest mood, mystery and ambience. This ambition works, I hope, in a poem such as Slieve Donard and The Clouds where both words and film can suggest the mystery and allure of the ever-changing sky.

The pictures were taken roughly over a ten-year period, from 2005 to2015, using Minolta cameras and Ilford HP5 and FP4 film. A debt of gratitude is owed to Steve Cawte, who worked with me patiently to transfer and position the images.

INDEX for purposes of identification, the photographs are aligned to the name of the poem they accompany.

Earthsong Frontspiece Ploughing below Slieve Binnian, Mourne Mountains, 2009.

The Shedding Gate Branding sheep, Mourne Mountains, 1966. (my father, centre)

The Bull Highland Bull below Slieve Meelmore, Mourne Mountains.

March Slemish Mountain, Co Antrim.

The Last of the Turf Cutters Cutting peat on the Gary Bog, Ballymoney 2011.

As if Gorse blossom on a mountain road above Attical, Co Down.

Slieve Donard and the Clouds (1) Slidderyford Dolmen, Dundrum and(2) The Mournes from outside Dundrum.

Plainsong Frontspiece Cloncha High Cross, near Culdaff, Co Donegal.

Psithurism Ancient rath, outside Broughshane, Co Antrim.

The Broad Stone Dolmen on The Long Mountain, Dunloy, Co Antrim.

Stowaway Maize field in cloches, Roselick, Portstewart.

Birdsong Frontspiece Ballywillwill Lake, near Castlewellan, Co Down.

Evensong Frontspiece Corn stooks, Seaforde, Co

Down.

Knitting my father and mother, Samuel and Mabel Holmes ,1952. family albumn.

Calendars (1) Legananny Dolmen and the Mourne Mountains, looking south (2) Same dolmen looking north.

Lifetime Bellarena Registry Office,Magilligan, 2005.

February Snowdrops, Benvarden Estate, Dervock, Co Antrim.

Pages of the Sea, Murlough. Irish soldier in the uniform of the British Army, circa 1918. Military Re - enactment, Portrush 2008.

Dogged Sculpture at the Dog Leap, Roe Valley Country Park, Limavady.

Something about September Cutting corn(oats) with a Ferguson tractor and binder. Glenshesk, Ballycastle, 2010. (2images).

Amongst the Ancients Corn stooks, Seaforde, Co Down.

The Road to Nowhere Deserted farmstead, Slieve Croob area, Co Down, winter and summer views.

ABOUT THE AUTHOR

Robin Holmes grew up on a small hill farm in the Mourne Mountains, an experience which he believes was both formative and nurturing for his later writing. He moved to Coleraine in 1972, where he studied English Literature and Philosophy at the New University of Ulster. He later embarked on a career in social work, working mainly in the Mental Health field.

After retirement he enrolled in Bernie McGill's Creative writing Class at Flowerfield Arts Centre, in Portstewart, Northern Ireland. This was a stimulus to a more sustained period of writing. Since 2018 a number of his poems have appeared in the Bangor Literary Journal. In 2020 his poem, As If, came fourth in their Annual Poetry Competition after a public on line vote. In 2021 and 2022 he was shortlisted for the Bangor Forty Words Competition. Outdoor location recordings of his poems, Psithurism and Fred Dibnah, are available on the Bangor Literary Journal's YouTube Channel.

Robin has also had his poems published in the Community Arts Partnership Poetry in Motion anthologies for the last six consecutive years. A contributor to the last three anthologies by the North

Coast Writers, his poem Heartfelt, appeared in the 2023 Anthology, Love, Loss and Cardiac Issues, published by Impspired Press.

He has given readings of his work in many venues, including The Seamus Heaney Homeplace and Flowerfield Arts Centre. An audio recording of his short story, The Iron Horse, is now part of the permanent exhibition for The Sam Henry Collection held by Causeway Coast and Glens Borough Council.

As this collection indicates he is also a keen photographer, working often with black and white film. As well as enjoying playing the guitar and mandola, he is still actively involved with the farming community, using his collection of vintage machinery regularly at harvest time.

Printed in Great Britain
by Amazon

38646441R00069